This journal belongs to

....

Date

....

God Made Teachers Special

On the sixth day, God created men and women.
On the seventh day, He rested. Not so much to recuperate,
but rather to prepare Himself for the work He was going to do
on the next day. For it was on that day—the eighth day—
that God created the first Teacher.

This Teacher, though taken from among men and women,
had several significant modifications. In general,
God made the Teacher more durable than other men
and women. He made the Teacher tough...but gentle, too.
Into the Teacher God poured a generous amount of patience.
He gave the Teacher a heart slightly bigger than
the average human heart. And He gave the Teacher
an abundant supply of hope.

When God finished creating the Teacher, He stepped back
and admired the work of His hands. And God saw that
the Teacher was good. Very good! And God smiled,
for when He looked at the Teacher, He saw into the future.
He was placing the future in the hands of the Teacher.

And because God loves Teachers so much,
on the ninth day God created "snow days."

I thank my God upon every remembrance of you.

PHILIPPIANS 1:3 KJV

Perspective

The measure of your real success
is one you cannot spend—
it's the way [a] child describes you
when talking to a friend.

MARTIN BAXBAUM

God made my life complete when I placed
all the pieces before him…. God rewrote the text
of my life when I opened the book of my heart to his eyes.

PSALM 18:20, 24 THE MSG

Kids don't care what you think until they think you care.

The tender loving care of human beings
will never become obsolete. People,
even more than things, have to be restored,
renewed, revived, reclaimed, and redeemed.
Never throw anybody out.

SAM LEVENSON

It is a special gift to be able
to view the world through
the eyes of a child.

Shaped by Love

Teaching is sharing ourselves with others.
We get the best from our students
when we give the best of ourselves.

Teaching is one of the few professions that permit love.

THEODORE ROETHKE

LORD, You are our Father. We are the clay,
and you are the potter.
We are all formed by your hand.

ISAIAH 64:8 NLT

Some people are so special that once they enter your life,
it becomes richer and fuller and more wonderful
than you ever thought it could be.

When my hands mold the clay of this child's life,
may the impressions be, in reality, made by the movement
of Your hands and directed by Your perfect thoughts.

GLORIA GAITHER

Every child is shaped in and by the mind of God.

The Light of Understanding

Have you ever been at sea in a dense fog,
when it seemed as if a tangible white darkness
shut you in and the great ship, tense and anxious,
groped her way toward the shore with plummet
and sounding line, and you waited with beating heart
for something to happen? I was like that ship before
my education began, only I was without compass
or sounding line, and no way of knowing how
near the harbor was. "Light! Give me light!"
was the wordless cry of my soul, and the light of love
shone on me in that very hour…. I have always
thought it would be a blessing if each person could
be blind and deaf for a few days during his early adult life.
Darkness would make him appreciate sight;
silence would teach him the joys of sound.

HELEN KELLER

*It is you who light my lamp; the LORD,
my God, lights up my darkness.*

PSALM 18:28 NRSV

Eyes to See

There is no satisfaction in the world that can compare
with seeing the light of understanding in a child's eyes.

MARGARET PERRY TEUFEL

Every day we live is a priceless gift of God,
loaded with possibilities to learn something new,
to gain fresh insights.

DALE EVANS ROGERS

Your word is a lamp to guide my feet and a light for my path.

PSALM 119:105 NLT

There is much satisfaction in work well done;
praise is sweet, but there can be no happiness equal to
the joy of finding a heart that understands.

VICTOR ROBINSON

When teachers let their love shine through,
their students are ready to learn.

*May God give you eyes to see beauty
only the heart can understand.*

The Light that Leads

Enthusiasm is the element of success in everything.
It is the light that leads and the strength that lifts people
on and up in the great struggles of scientific pursuits
and of professional labor. It robs endurance of difficulty,
and makes duty a pleasure.

BISHOP DOANE

Send out your light and your truth;
let them guide me.

PSALM 43:3 NLT

What other profession offers one the satisfaction
of knowing you have lit a spark in the mind of
the next generation and nurtured a fire that
will burn long after you've gone?

RAE ELLEN McKEE

If you follow me, you won't have to
walk in darkness, because you will
have the light that leads to life.

JOHN 8:12 NLT

A Private Hope

Teaching is not a job, but a way of life.
If you have a zest for living,
and are a cheerleader for life,
then the teaching profession is for you....
Being surrounded by the enthusiasm of youth,
you will be able to continue to experience
the wonders of learning through
your students' endeavors. Your creative juices
will know no bounds, and you will have
the freedom to allow your students to dream,
as you help guide them toward their dreams.

MARILYN BLACK

Let us think of education as the means of
developing our greatest abilities,
because in each of us there is a private hope
and dream which, fulfilled,
can be translated into benefit for everyone
and greater strength for our nation.

JOHN F. KENNEDY

I came so they can have real and eternal life,
more and better life than they ever dreamed of.

JOHN 10:10 MSG

To Dream

To dream anything that you want to dream:
that is the beauty of the human mind.
To do anything that you want to do:
that is the strength of the human will.
To trust yourself to test your limits:
that is the courage to succeed.

BERNARD EDMONDS

Do not pray for dreams equal to your powers.
Pray for powers equal to your dreams.

ADELAIDE ANN PROCTER

There are no limits to our opportunities.
Most of us see only a small portion of what is possible.
We create opportunities by seeing the possibilities
and having the persistence to act upon them.
We must always remember...opportunities are always here,
but we must look for them.

....

....

....

....

....

....

God can do anything, you know—
far more than you could ever imagine or guess
or request in your wildest dreams!

EPHESIANS 3:20 MSG

Dream-Makers

It's a thrill to fulfill your own childhood dreams,
but as you get older you may find that enabling
the dreams of others is even more fun.

RANDY PAUSCH

When dreams come true, there is life and joy.

PROVERBS 13:12 TLB

My teaching mission is to be a dream-maker
for my students, not a dream-breaker.
To dream is to be filled with hope.
I know this because I see the faces of hope daily.

CHAUNCEY VEATCH

You are the molders of their dreams...
the spark that sets aflame the poet's hand
or lights the flame in some great singer's song.

CLARK MOLLENHOFF

....

....

....

....

....

....

Only dreamers can teach us to soar.

ANNE MARIE PIERCE

Entrusted with the Future

The future of the world is in my classroom today,
a future with the potential for good or bad....
Several future presidents are learning from me today;
so are the great writers of the next decades,
and so are all the so-called ordinary people
who will make the decisions in a democracy.
I must never forget these same young people
could be the thieves and murderers of the future.
Only a teacher? Thank God I have a calling
to the greatest profession of all! I must be vigilant
every day, lest I lose one fragile opportunity
to improve tomorrow.

Ivan Welton Fitzwater

When he, the Spirit of truth, comes,
he will guide you into all the truth.

JOHN 16:13 NIV

Touch the Future

Live for today but hold your hands open to tomorrow.
Anticipate the future and its changes with joy.
There is a seed of God's love in every event,
every circumstance, every unpleasant situation
in which you may find yourself.

BARBARA JOHNSON

Neither the present nor the future, nor any powers,
neither height nor depth, nor anything else in all creation,
will be able to separate us from the love of God.

ROMANS 8:38–39 NIV

Lord...give me the gift of faith to be renewed
and shared with others each day. Teach me to live
this moment only, looking neither to the past
with regret, nor the future with apprehension.
Let love be my aim and my life a prayer.

ROSEANN ALEXANDER-ISHAM

I touch the future; I teach.

CHRISTA MCAULIFFE

Plans for Hope

Teaching children involves helping them
shape their ambitions and their sense of personal destiny.

GORDON MACDONALD

I'll show my children right from wrong,
encourage dreams and hope;
explain respect for others,
while teaching them to cope
with outside pressures, inside fears,
a world that's less than whole;
and through it all I'll nurture
my children's most precious soul!
Though oftentimes a struggle,
this job I'll never trade;
for in my hand tomorrow lives…
a future God has made.

....
....
....
....
....
....
....
....
....
....
....
....
....
....
....
....
....
....

"For I know the plans I have for you,"
declares the LORD, "plans to prosper
you and not to harm you, plans to give
you hope and a future."

JEREMIAH 29:11 NIV

Press On

Nothing in the world can take the place of persistence.
Talent will not; nothing is more common
than unsuccessful men with talent. Genius will not;
unrewarded genius is almost a proverb.
Education will not; the world is full of educated derelicts.
Persistence and determination are omnipotent.
The slogan "press on" has solved and always
will solve the problems of the human race.
No person was ever honored for what he received.
Honor has been the reward for what he gave.

CALVIN COOLIDGE

I press on toward the goal to win the prize
for which God has called me.

PHILIPPIANS 3:14 NIV

....

....

....

....

....

....

....

....

The world will always need teachers like you—
so understanding, so helpful, so caring.
Thanks for not giving up on me!

The Success of Persistence

Persistent people begin their success
where others end in failure.

EDWARD EGGLESTON

Success is failure turned inside out,
The silver tint of the clouds of doubt,
And you never can tell how close you are,
It may be near when it seems so far.
So stick to the fight when you're hardest hit,
It's when things seem worst,
That you must not quit.

I can do all things through Christ
who strengthens me.

PHILIPPIANS 4:13 NKJV

*To those who by persistence in doing good
seek glory, honor and immortality,
he will give eternal life.*

ROMANS 2:7 NIV

Opportunities Disguised

We are continually faced by great
opportunities brilliantly disguised as insoluble problems.

'Tis a lesson you should heed,
Try, try again;
If at first you don't succeed,
Try, try again;
Then your courage should appear,
For, if you will persevere,
You will conquer, never fear;
Try, try again.

W. E. HICKSON

So be careful how you live....
Make the most of every opportunity.

EPHESIANS 5:15–16 NLT

Life's great opportunities often open
on the road of daily duties.

....
....
....
....
....
....

In teaching you cannot see the fruit of a day's work. It is invisible and remains so, maybe for twenty years.

JACQUES BARZUN

A Work of Heart

It is not the job that determines its worth
and impact, rather the heart of the person
approaching and executing the task.
No work in itself is spiritual or secular.

JEAN FLEMING

Love is patient, love is kind...; bears all things,
believes all things, hopes all things,
endures all things. Love never fails.

1 CORINTHIANS 13:4, 7-8 NASB

Far and away the best prize that life offers
is the chance to work hard at work worth doing.

THEODORE ROOSEVELT

Let your words be tender and caressing...
discipline that wins the heart's assent.

ELIJAH BEN SOLOMON ZALMAN

The best teachers teach from the heart, not from the book.

The Essence of Teaching

If I were to make a solemn speech
in praise of you, in gratitude, in deep affection,
you would turn an alarming shade of crimson
and try to escape. So I won't. Take it all as said.

MARION C. GARRETTY

When I approach a child,
he inspires in me two sentiments:
tenderness for what he is,
and respect for what he may become.

LOUIS PASTEUR

My goal is that they may be
encouraged in heart and united in love,
so that they may have the full riches
of complete understanding.

COLOSSIANS 2:2 NIV

....

....

....

....

....

....

....

The essence of teaching is to make learning contagious, to have one idea spark another.

MARVA COLLINS

Captivating

You can never go home without
a smile on your face when you teach kids.
I was always beaming at the end of the day.
And it was so inspirational each morning
to see that the kids were excited to be back at school....
I still cannot get used to how much my heart soars
with every student's success, and how a piece of my heart
is plucked away when any student slips away.

DELISSA L. MAI

O dearest [child], My heart for better lore
would seldom yearn,
could I but teach the hundredth part of what
from thee I learn.

WILLIAM WORDSWORTH

....

....

....

....

....

....

....

....

To reach a child's mind a teacher must capture his heart. Only if a child feels right can he think right.

HAIM G. GINOTT

To Make the World a Better Place

You've made me a better person.
Wherever I may go in my life,
I will always remember that I had an excellent guide
in the form of a teacher: You!

Do what you can to show you care about other people,
and you will make our world a better place.

ROSALYNN CARTER

There is a latent desire in every human being
to do something of worth that will have lasting significance...
something that will make life better for others.

TONY CAMPOLO

In my belief, you cannot deal with
the most serious things in the world unless you
also understand the most amusing.

SIR WINSTON CHURCHILL

....

....

....

....

....

*W*hile we have opportunity,
let us do good to all people.

GALATIANS 6:10 NASB

Influence

Whoever first coined the phrase
"you're the wind beneath my wings"
most assuredly was reflecting
on the sublime influence of a very special teacher.

FRANK TRUJILLO

Never underestimate the influence of a caring teacher.

The highest excellence which an individual can attain
must be to work according to the best of his genius
and to work in harmony with God's creation.

J. H. SMYTH

The smallest good deed is better than the grandest intention.

Face the work of every day with the influence
of a few thoughtful, quiet moments with your heart and God.

L. B. COWMAN

....

....

....

....

....

....

*Their good deeds will be remembered forever.
They will have influence and honor.*

PSALM 112:9 NLT

A Wise Adventure

One hundred years from now
it will not matter what kind of car I drove,
what kind of house I lived in,
or how much money I had in the bank.
One hundred years from now
it will not matter what kind of computer I used,
what kind of school I attended,
or how many degrees I had.
But the world will be a little better,
because I was important in the life of a child.

Teach us to number our days,
That we may present to You a heart of wisdom.

PSALM 90:12 NASB

Open your eyes, your ears, your mind, your heart, your spirit and you'll find adventure everywhere.

WILFERD A. PETERSON

An Honored Calling

What constitutes success?
They have achieved success who have lived well;
laughed often and loved much;
who have gained the respect of intelligent people
and the love of little children;
who have filled their niche and accomplished their task;
who have left the world better than they found it,
whether by an improved poppy,
a perfect poem or a rescued soul;
who have never lacked appreciation of
earth's beauty, or failed to express it;
who have always looked for the best in others
and given the best they had;
whose life was an inspiration;
whose memory a benediction.

BESSIE ANDERSON STANLEY

*To this you were called so that you
may inherit a blessing.*

1 Peter 3:9 NIV

Call of the Heart

Teaching is a calling, not a choice.

MARY ANN ALEXANDER

There's no word in the language
I revere more than "teacher." My heart sings
when a kid refers to me as his teacher,
and it always has. I've honored myself
and the entire family of man by becoming a teacher.

PAT CONROY

I pray that the eyes of your heart may be
enlightened in order that you may know
the hope to which he has called you.

EPHESIANS 1:18 NIV

We are not called by God to extraordinary things,
but to do ordinary things with extraordinary love.

JEAN VANIER

*Dedicate yourself to the call of your heart
and see where it leads you.*

The Joy of Teaching

We find our greatest joy, not in getting,
but in expressing what we are.
We do not really live for honors or for pay;
our gladness is not in the taking and holding,
but in the doing, the striving, the building,
the living. It is a higher joy to teach than to be taught....
The happy person is the one who lives the life of love,
not for the honors it may bring, but for the life itself.

R. J. Baughan

There is no greater pleasure than bringing
to the uncluttered, supple mind of a child
the delight of knowing God and the many
rich things He has given us to enjoy.

Gladys M. Hunt

....

....

....

....

....

....

....

....

....

....

....

....

....

....

....

....

*Y*our job is to teach them the rules
and instructions, to show them
how to live, what to do.

EXODUS 18:20 MSG

The Power of One

There is not enough darkness in all the world
to put out the light of one small candle....
In moments of discouragement, defeat,
or even despair, there are always
certain things to cling to. Little things usually:
remembered laughter, the face of a sleeping child,
a tree in the wind—in fact, any reminder of
something deeply felt or dearly loved.
No man is so poor as not to have many
of these small candles. When they are lighted,
darkness goes away and a touch of wonder remains.

SIR ARTHUR GORDON

The one who blesses others is abundantly blessed;
those who help others are helped.

PROVERBS 11:25 MSG

....

....

....

....

....

....

....

....

....

....

....

....

....

....

....

....

....

....

*Let us think of ways to motivate one another
to acts of love and good works.*

HEBREWS 10:24 NLT

Unique Gift

You have a unique message to deliver,
a unique song to sing, a unique act of love to bestow.
This message, this song, and this act of love
have been entrusted exclusively to the one and only you.

JOHN POWELL

What happens when we live God's way?
He brings gifts into our lives, much the same way
that fruit appears in an orchard—
things like affection for others,
exuberance about life, serenity.
We develop a willingness to stick with things,
a sense of compassion in the heart.

GALATIANS 5:22–23 MSG

Live your life while you have it. Life is a
splendid gift—there is nothing small about it.

FLORENCE NIGHTINGALE

Gifts of Value

I teach little children to read.
I hold the values of our culture and the history
of our world before them like a sweet confection....
I possess the power to lace their intake with arsenic
or sweet nectar, creating their self-esteem
or destroying it. I shudder under the burden of such
a responsibility.... However, where it is always
appropriate to hold teachers accountable for
doing their job, which is teaching, it is not
always possible to hold them responsible
for doing the student's job, which is learning.

RAE ELLEN McKEE

Are not five sparrows sold for two copper coins?
And not one of them is forgotten before God.
But the very hairs of your head are all numbered.
Do not fear therefore; you are of more
value than many sparrows.

LUKE 12:6–7 NKJV

*Teach me, Father, to value each day,
to live, to love, to laugh, to play.*

KATHY MILLS

Work through Weakness

Tending to the weakest among us teaches us
the power of true strength.

CHRISTOPHER DE VINCK

How do I love God?... By doing beautifully
the work I have been given to do, by doing simply
that which God has entrusted to me,
in whatever form it may take.

MOTHER TERESA

There's no thrill in easy sailing when the skies are clear and blue,
There's no joy in merely doing things which any one can do.
But there is some satisfaction that is mighty sweet to take,
when you reach a destination that you thought you'd never make.

My grace is sufficient for you, for My strength is made perfect in weakness.

2 CORINTHIANS 12:9 NKJV

Discovering Gifts

It is my belief that God gives us all gifts,
special abilities that we have the privilege of
developing to help us serve Him and humanity.

BENJAMIN CARSON

I determined that there should not be
a minute in the day when my children should not be
aware by my face and my lips that my heart
was theirs, that their happiness was my
happiness and their pleasures my pleasures.

JOHANN HEINRICH PESTALOZZI

Each one of us is God's special work of art.
Through us, He teaches and inspires,
delights and encourages, informs and uplifts
all those who view our lives.

JONI EARECKSON TADA

Once we discover how to appreciate the timeless values in our daily experiences, we can enjoy the best things in life.

This Is the Day

God give me joy in the common things:
In the dawn that lures, the eve that sings.
In the new grass sparkling after rain,
In the late wind's wild and weird refrain;
In the springtime's spacious field of gold,
In the precious light by winter doled....
In the songs of children, unrestrained;
In the sober wisdom age has gained.
God give me joy in the tasks that press,
In the memories that burn and bless;
In the thought that life has love to spend,
In the faith that God's at journey's end.

THOMAS CURTIS CLARK

....

....

....

....

....

....

....

....

This is the day the LORD has made;
We will rejoice and be glad in it.

PSALM 118:24 NKJV

Each New Day

Today is unique! It has never occurred before
and it will never be repeated.
At midnight it will end, quietly,
suddenly, totally. Forever.
But the hours between now and then
are opportunities with eternal possibilities.

CHARLES R. SWINDOLL

No other job offers you the opportunity
to be in control of your own daily plan,
and to work in an environment where
every day is different. Because you will be
working with youth, routine is non-existent
and each day will present new challenges.

MARILYN BLACK

At the end of each day, she would tell the class,
"Remember, tomorrow is a new day. If you've made mistakes
today, you can have a fresh start." I think she would be surprised
to know how powerfully that thought has affected my life.

....

....

....

....

....

All the days ordained for me were written in your book before one of them came to be.

PSALM 139:16 NIV

The Miracle of a Day

This bright, new day, complete with 24 hours
of opportunities, choices, and attitudes
comes with a perfectly matched set of 1,440 minutes.
This unique gift, this one day, cannot be exchanged,
replaced or refunded. Handle with care.
Make the most of it. There is only one to a customer!

Show me your ways, LORD,
teach me your paths.... You are God my Savior,
and my hope is in you all day long.

PSALM 25:4-5 NIV

Each of my days are miracles.
I won't waste my day;
I won't throw away a miracle.

KELLEY VICKSTROM

....

....

....

....

....

....

....

....

Better than a thousand days of diligent study is one day with a great teacher.

JAPANESE PROVERB

Words of Praise

Encouragement is awesome. It has the capacity
to lift a man's or woman's shoulders.
To spark the flicker of a smile on the face
of a discouraged child. To breathe fresh fire
into the fading embers of a smoldering dream.
To actually change the course
of another human being's day, week, or life.

CHARLES R. SWINDOLL

I try to make it possible for all my students
to have a chance to be successful at tasks
that suit their talents and to see that
someone loves them and cares about
what they accomplish. I personally invite
all my students to become active
participants in their own learning.

BRUCE E. BROMBACHER

....
....
....
....
....
....
....
....
....
....
....
....
....
....
....
....
....
....
....
....
....
....
....

Encourage the disheartened, help the weak,
be patient with everyone.

1 THESSALONIANS 5:14 NIV

An Encouraging Word

There are times when encouragement means such a lot.
And a word is enough to convey it.

GRACE STRICKER DAWSON

People have a way of becoming
what you encourage them to be.

SCUDDER N. PARKER

Affection is the most satisfying reward
a child can receive. It costs nothing,
is readily available, and provides great encouragement.
I'll show these children right from wrong,
encourage dreams and hope; explain respect for others,
while teaching them to cope with outside pressures,
inside fears, a world that's less than whole;
and through it all I'll nurture each child's
most precious soul! Though oftentimes a struggle,
this job I'll never trade; for in my hand
tomorrow lives...a future God has made.

....

....

....

....

....

....

May God who gives patience, steadiness, and encouragement help you to live in complete harmony with each other.

ROMANS 15:5 TLB

With Understanding

When we really love others,
we accept them as they are.
We make our love visible through
little acts of kindness, shared activities,
words of praise and thanks,
and our willingness to get along with them.

EDWARD E. FORD

My teacher, how can I ever thank you enough?
What you have given me will stay with me a lifetime.
Thank you for believing in me,
for teaching me with patience and understanding.

CATHERINE PULSIFER

Encouragement is being a good listener,
being positive, letting others know you accept them
for who they are. It is offering hope,
caring about the feelings of another,
understanding.

GIGI GRAHAM TCHIVIDJIAN

Timely advice is lovely,
like golden apples in a silver basket.

PROVERBS 25:11 NLT

Remember that You're Needed

With a special gift for learning
And with a heart that deeply cares,
You add a lot of love
To everything you share.
And even though you mean a lot,
You'll never know how much,
For you helped to change the world
Through every life you touched.
You sparked the creativity
In the students whom you taught
And helped them to strive for goals,
For dreams that can't be bought.
You are such a special teacher
That no words can truly tell
How very much you're valued
For the work you do so well.

Remember that you are needed. There is at least one important
work to be done that will not be done unless you do it.

CHARLES L. ALLEN

And let the loveliness of our Lord, our God,
rest on us, confirming the work that we do.

PSALM 90:17 MSG

Build a Foundation

You're a foundation builder....
What could be more important
than helping to shape and mold others' lives?

GUY RICE DOUD

Because of God's grace to me,
I have laid the foundation like an expert builder.
Now others are building on it. But whoever is building
on this foundation must be very careful.

1 CORINTHIANS 3:10 NLT

If a child is to keep his inborn sense of wonder...
he needs the companionship of at least one adult
who can share it, rediscovering with him the joy,
excitement, and mystery of the world we live in.

RACHEL CARSON

*What is important is not what you do
as a teacher, but what your students learn
as a result of what you do.*

HOWARD HENDRICKS

Joyful Work

Teachers teach because they care.
Teaching young people is what they do best.
It requires long hours, patience, and care.

Horace Mann

Caring teachers are among our nation's greatest treasures;
they are entrusted with its future.

Half the joy of life is in little things taken on the run.
Let us run if we must—even the sands do that—
but let us keep our hearts young and our eyes open
that nothing worth our while shall escape us.
And everything is worth its while
if we only grasp it and its significance.

Victor Cherbuliez

....

....

....

....

....

....

....

To enjoy your work...is indeed a gift from God.
The person who does that will not
need to look back with sorrow on his
past, for God gives him joy.

ECCLESIASTES 5:20 TLB

Small Daily Differences

When you thought I wasn't looking,
you gave me a sticker, and I knew that little things
were special things. When you thought
I wasn't looking, you put your arm around me,
and I felt loved. When you thought I wasn't looking,
I saw tears come from your eyes, and I learned that
sometimes things hurt—but that it's alright to cry....
When you thought I wasn't looking, you cared,
and I wanted to be everything I could be.
When you thought I wasn't looking—I looked...
and wanted to say thanks for all those things
you did when you thought I wasn't looking.

MARY RITA SCHILKE KORZAN

Work willingly at whatever you do,
as though you were working for the Lord
rather than for people.

COLOSSIANS 3:23 NLT

....

....

....

....

....

....

My teacher thought I was smarter than I was; so I was.

SIX-YEAR-OLD STUDENT

To Love a Child

A child, unlike any other, yet identical
to all those who have preceded and all who will follow,
sits in a classroom today—hopeful, enthusiastic, curious.
The touch of a teacher will make the difference!

SHARON M. DRAPER

To love [a child] is to bring out the best in him,
to teach him to love what is difficult.

NADIA BOULANGER

Choices can change our lives profoundly.
The choice to mend a broken relationship,
to say "yes" to a difficult assignment,
to lay aside some important work to play with a child,
to visit some forgotten person—these small
choices may affect many lives eternally.

GLORIA GAITHER

Most children need more love than they deserve.

Whoever welcomes a little child like this in my name welcomes me.

MATTHEW 18:5 NIV

Little Things

God, Your heart is the most sensitive and tender of all.
No act goes unnoticed, no matter
how insignificant or small....
Thank You for paying attention to small things.
Thank You for valuing the insignificant....
Thank You far caring about me.

RICHARD J. FOSTER

Thank You, God, for little things
That often come our way,
The things we take for granted
But don't mention when we pray.
The unexpected courtesy,
The thoughtful kindly deed,
A hand reached out to help us
In the time of sudden need.
Oh, make us more aware, dear God,
Of little daily graces
That come to us with sweet surprise
From never-dreamed-of places.

*You become great by accepting,
not asserting. Your spirit, not your size,
makes the difference.*

Luke 9:48 msg

The Brave

Only the brave should teach.
Only those who love the young should teach.
Teaching is a vocation. It is as sacred
as the priesthood; as innate as a desire,
as inescapable as the genius which compels
a great artist. If one has not the concern
for humanity, the love of living creatures,
the vision of the priest and the artist,
one must not teach.

PEARL S. BUCK

I would be true, for there are those who trust me;
I would be pure, for there are those who care;
I would be strong, for there is much to suffer;
I would be brave, for there is much to dare.

HOWARD ARNOLD WALTER

God is a safe place to hide, ready to help when we need him. We stand fearless at the cliff-edge of doom, courageous in seastorm and earthquake.

PSALM 46:1-2 MSG

Dare to Believe

The work in front of you is God's work and not yours.
If God wants it to succeed, it will.
If God doesn't, it won't.
What God wants of you is to try!
So have courage—and move.

IGNATIUS OF LOYOLA

Wait patiently for the LORD.
Be brave and courageous.

PSALM 27:14 NLT

Make no little plans; they have no magic
to stir [the soul] and probably themselves
will not be realized. Make big plans;
aim high in hope and work,
remembering that a noble,
logical diagram once recorded will not die.

DANIEL H. BURNHAM

You have a special way of caring and bringing
out the best in all your students.
Thanks for daring to believe the best of us.

The Strength of Love

Dare to love and to be a real friend.
The love you give and receive is a reality
that will lead you closer and closer to God
as well as to those whom God has given you to love.

HENRI J. M. NOUWEN

Do not fear, for I am with you;
Do not anxiously look about you, for I am your God.
I will strengthen you, surely I will help you,
Surely I will uphold you with My righteous right hand.

ISAIAH 41:10 NASB

God, grant me wisdom,
Grant me vision,
Grant me courage,
Grant me love,
To teach a child.

IDA NELLE HOLLAWAY

*There is no fear in love;
but perfect love casts out fear.*

1 JOHN 4:18 NKJV

An Awakener

God is able to bless you abundantly,
so that in all things at all times, having all that you need,
you will abound in every good work.

2 Corinthians 9:8 niv

The task of the excellent teacher is to stimulate
"apparently ordinary" people to unusual effort.
The tough problem is not in identifying winners:
it is in making winners out of ordinary people.

K. Patricia Cross

The art of the creative teacher is to awaken
the natural curiosity of eager young minds.

Life begets life. Energy creates energy.
It is by spending oneself that one becomes rich.

Sarah Bernhardt

I am not a teacher...I am an awakener.

ROBERT FROST

A Gift of Enthusiasm

Whatever you do, put romance and enthusiasm
into the lives of our children.

MARGARET R. MacDONALD

I studied the lives of great men and famous women,
and I found that the men and women who got
to the top were those who did the jobs they had
in hand with everything they had of energy
and enthusiasm and hard work.

HARRY S. TRUMAN

I don't dream of wealth and success for you.
But instead, a job you like, skills you can perfect,
enthusiasm to lighten your heart,
friends, and love in abundance.

PAM BROWN

Enthusiasm is a kind of faith that has been set on fire.

GEORGE MATTHEW ADAMS

Don't you see that children are God's best gift?... His generous legacy?

PSALM 127:3 MSG

The Power of Imagination

The huge dome of the sky is of all things
sensuously perceived the most like infinity.
When God made space and worlds
that move in space, and clothed our world with air,
and gave us such eyes and such imaginations
as those we have, He knew what the sky would mean to us....
We cannot be certain that this was not indeed one
of the chief purposes for which Nature was created.

C. S. Lewis

God can do anything, you know—
far more than you could ever imagine
or guess or request in your wildest dreams!

Ephesians 3:20 msg

A child is...an island of curiosity
surrounded by a sea of question marks.

The imagination should be allowed a certain amount of time to browse around.

THOMAS MERTON

Thankful

Thanks for...
making the difference
long, long hours
creating a sense of family
being the keeper of dreams
using good judgment
teaching for learning
making reading fun
forgiving
being the wind beneath my wings
that sensitive touch
never giving up on anybody
believing in miracles
respecting each other
taking responsibility for all students
keeping a tight rein on discipline
striving for excellence, not perfection
being brave
smiling a lot
never depriving our children of hope.

....

....

....

....

....

You're my hero! I will always be thankful to you, my teacher, for all the hard work and effort you have invested in my education.

A Noble Task

I long to accomplish a great and noble task,
but it is my chief duty to accomplish humble tasks
as though they were great and noble.
The world is moved along, not only by
the mighty shoves of its heroes, but also by the aggregate
of the tiny pushes of each honest worker.

HELEN KELLER

It is in your daily work, whether you are
keeping books, making sales, teaching school,
building bridges, driving a truck....
Think of whatever you are doing as an adventure
and watch your life change for the better.

WILFERD A. PETERSON

Just as there are no little people or unimportant lives,
there is no insignificant work.

ELENA BONNER

*The noble make noble plans,
and by noble deeds they stand.*

ISAIAH 32:8 NIV

Unsung Heroes

In our world of big names, curiously our true heroes
tend to be anonymous. In this life of illusion
and quasi-illusion, the person of solid virtues
who can be admired for something more substantial
than his well-knownness often proves to be
the unsung hero: the teacher, the nurse, the mother,
the honest cop, the hard worker at lonely, underpaid,
unglamorous, unpublicized jobs.

DANIEL J. BOORSTIN

God has given each of you some special abilities;
be sure to use them to help each other,
passing on to others God's many kinds of blessings.

1 PETER 4:10 TLB

....

....

....

....

....

....

....

....

*Nurture your mind with great thoughts;
to believe in the heroic makes heroes.*

BENJAMIN DISRAELI

Learn to Laugh

If you can learn to laugh in spite of the circumstances
that surround you, you will enrich others, enrich yourself,
and more than that, you will last!

BARBARA JOHNSON

If you'll promise not to believe everything
your child says happens at school,
I'll promise not to believe everything
he says happens at home.

A NOTE TO PARENTS

Children are unpredictable. You never know
what inconsistency they're going to catch you in next.

FRANKLIN P. JONES

A keen sense of humor helps us to overlook the unbecoming,
understand the unconventional, tolerate the unpleasant,
overcome the unexpected, and outlast the unbearable.

BILLY GRAHAM

....

....

....

....

....

....

A merry heart does good, like medicine.

PROVERBS 17:22 NKJV

Real Joy

The real joy of life is in its play.
Play is anything we do for the joy and love of doing it,
apart from any profit, compulsion, or sense of duty.
It is the real living of life with the feeling of freedom
and self-expression. Play is the business of childhood,
and its continuation in later years is the prolongation of youth.

WALTER RAUSCHENBUSCH

Laughter dulls the sharpest pain and flattens
out the greatest stress. To share it is to give a gift
of health because, as someone pointed out,
"Ulcers can't grow while you're laughing."

HUNTER "PATCH" ADAMS

Let all who take refuge in You be glad,
Let them ever sing for joy.

PSALM 5:11 NASB

Embrace Humor

Teachers have to: stand above all their students,
yet be on their level; be able to do 180 other things
not connected with the subject they teach;
run on coffee, Cokes, and leftovers;
communicate vital knowledge to thousands
of students daily and be right; have as much,
and sometimes more, time for the job as they
do for themselves; and have a smile that
can endure everything from practical jokes to referendum votes.
Teachers are an absolute miracle.

Laugh at yourself. You will always be
your greatest source of humor. Don't ever
take yourself so seriously that you can't find humor
in the things you say and do.

BRUCE BICKLE AND STAN JANTZ

....

....

....

....

....

....

....

....

The joy of the Lord is your strength.

Nehemiah 8:10 tlb

Classroom Management

A schoolteacher injured his back
and had to wear a plaster cast around his torso.
It fit under his shirt and was not noticeable at all.
On the first day of the term, still with the cast
under his shirt, he found himself assigned to
the toughest students in school. Walking confidently
into the rowdy classroom, he opened the window
as wide as possible and then busied himself
with desk work. When a strong breeze made
his tie flap, he took the desk stapler and stapled the tie
to his chest. He had no trouble with discipline that term.

Some people regard discipline as a chore.
For me, it's a kind of order that sets me free to fly.

JULIE ANDREWS

The LORD *corrects those he loves,*
just as a father corrects a child
in whom he delights.

PROVERBS 3:12 NLT

Diligence

A child is...such a knot of little purposeful nature!

RICHARD EBERHART

Learning is not attained by chance,
it must be sought with ardor
and attended to with diligence.

ABIGAIL ADAMS

I love those who love me [wisdom];
And those who diligently seek me will find me.

PROVERBS 8:17 NASB

It's time to get back to some old-fashioned values,
like commitment and sacrifice and responsibility
and purity and love.... Not only will our children
benefit from our self-discipline and perseverance,
but we adults will live in a less neurotic world, too!

JAMES DOBSON

That energy which makes a child hard
to manage is the energy which afterward
makes him a manager of life.

HENRY WARD BEECHER

Respect Is Earned

When I taught in public high school for three years
I always ate lunch with a different group of students,
whether they were in my class or not,
until I got to know most of them.
The teachers thought I was idiotic,
but they didn't realize that it actually
made it easier for me to teach,
that before I could effectively discipline students,
I had to earn their friendship and respect.

MARVA COLLINS

Don't demand respect....
Demand civility and insist on honesty.
Respect is something you must earn—
with kids as well as with adults.

Let everything you say be good and helpful,
so that your words will be an encouragement
to those who hear them.

EPHESIANS 4:29 NLT

A Passion for Knowledge

When you stood in front of our class,
I could see that you not only cared about us,
but you cared deeply about what
you were communicating, and it was contagious.
Thank you for teaching with passion.

Love for passing on knowledge,
for the fire that burns in the child
who understands and the recognition
of a mind opened, is a priceless gift....
When I see a young person who has
a burning love for learning, a passion for
new ideas and life in general, a desire to help
others and thrive on challenges,
I know I am in the presence of a potential teacher.
I would recommend that this young person
enter the teaching profession because
only in teaching can we satisfy all of these ideals.

MARILYN JACHETTI WHIRRY

....

....

....

....

....

....

Teach me knowledge and good judgment,
for I trust your commands.

PSALM 119:66 NIV

The Wonder of a Story

Thought flows in terms of stories—
stories about events, stories about people,
and stories about intentions and achievements.
The best teachers are the best storytellers.
We learn in the form of stories.

FRANK SMITH

My greatest satisfaction as a teacher has been
helping young people learn to love history
and instilling in them a personal desire
to seek knowledge. I have always seen my
role as a teacher to facilitate student learning
in what will be a life-long quest for knowledge,
to help ignite in them the spark of enlightenment,
to motivate their interest, and to cultivate their minds.

PHILIP BIGLER

*For everything that was written
in the past was written to teach us.*

ROMANS 15:4 NIV

Find Purpose

The most important function of education at any level
is to develop the personality of the individual
and the significance of his life to himself and to others.

GRAYSON KIRK

There would be no sense in asking why
if one did not believe in anything.
The word itself presupposes purpose.
Purpose presupposes a powerful intelligence.
Somebody has to have been responsible.
It is because we believe in God
that we address questions to Him.

ELISABETH ELLIOT

Have a purpose in life, and having it,
throw into your work such strength of mind
and muscle as God has given you.

THOMAS CARLYLE

....

....

....

....

....

....

....

....

....

....

....

....

....

....

....

....

....

....

....

....

....

....

*I will instruct you...and guide you along
the best pathway for your life; I will advise
you and watch your progress.*

PSALM 32:8 TLB

Knowledge and Wisdom

Anyone who stops learning is old,
whether at twenty or eighty.
Anyone who keeps learning stays young.

HENRY FORD

Is life not full of opportunities for learning love?
Every man and woman every day has a thousand of them.
The world is not a playground, it is a schoolroom.
Life is not a holiday, but an education.
And the one eternal lesson for us all is how better we can love.

HENRY DRUMMOND

You have done many good things for me, LORD,
just as you promised. I believe in your commands;
now teach me good judgment and knowledge.

PSALM 119:65–66 NLT

Knowledge is proud that it knows so much;
wisdom is humble that it knows no more.

WILLIAM COWPER

To Teach Is to Learn

You can teach a student a lesson for a day;
but if you can teach him to learn
by creating curiosity, he will continue
the learning process as long as he lives.

CLAY P. BEDFORD

O God, You have taught me
from my earliest childhood,
and I constantly tell others about
the wonderful things you do.

PSALM 71:17 NLT

A person who doesn't know but knows that
he doesn't know is a student; teach him.
A person who knows but who doesn't know that
he knows is asleep; awaken him. But a person who knows
and knows that he knows is wise; follow him.

ASIAN PROVERB

....

....

....

....

....

....

....

....

....

....

....

....

....

....

....

*I was still learning when
I taught my last class.*

CLAUDE M. FUESS

More than Expected

Thanks for...
being tough-minded but tenderhearted
showing enthusiasm even when you don't feel like it
keeping your promises
giving your best
your wisdom and courage
being punctual and insisting on it in others
providing creative solutions
avoiding the negative and seeking out the good
being there when students need you
listening
doing more than is expected
never giving up on what you really want
remaining open, flexible, and curious
being a friend
sharing
keeping several irons in the fire
being a child's hero
going the distance
having a good sense of humor
being a dream maker
giving your heart.

....

....

....

....

*Do not neglect doing good and sharing,
for with such sacrifices God is pleased.*

HEBREWS 13:16 NASB

Planting Seeds

My first precept about teaching is to
accept every child entrusted to me
because each one is his parents' greatest gift.
It is my job to accept him as he is,
teach him what I must, and help him reach
a new and better understanding of himself
and the world in which he lives....
Teaching is a timeless profession.
It is the basis of all other professions.
Good teachers plant the seeds
that make good doctors, good accountants,
good public servants, good statesmen,
good taxi drivers and good astronauts.

MARY V. BICOUVARIS

Children are like wet cement.
Whatever falls on them makes an impression.

HAIM GINOTT

*To one who listens, valid criticism
is like a gold earring or other gold jewelry.*

PROVERBS 25:12 NLT

Verbal Trophies

Thanks for the push when I needed it
and for the encouragement to try every day.

A word of praise is a "verbal trophy,"
and every child has abundant shelf space for such honors.

JAN DARGATZ

Praise does wonders for our sense of hearing.

ARNOLD H. GLASGOW

A student never forgets an encouraging private word,
when it is given with sincere respect and admiration.

WILLIAM LYON PHELPS

Look for the best in each other,
and always do your best to bring it out.

Think on This

There is no medicine like hope,
no incentive so great, and no tonic so powerful
as expectation of something better tomorrow.

Whatever things are true, whatever things are noble,
whatever things are just, whatever things are pure,
whatever things are lovely, whatever things are
of good report, if there is any virtue,
and if there is anything praiseworthy—
meditate on these things.

PHILIPPIANS 4:8 NKJV

It is only by thinking about great and good things
that we come to love them, and it is only by loving them
that we come to long for them, and it is only by longing
for themthat we are impelled to seek after them;
and it is only by seeking after them that they become ours.

HENRY VAN DYKE

....

....

....

....

....

....

....

We live in the present, we dream of the future,
but we learn eternal truths from the past.

LUCY MAUD MONTGOMERY

The Art of Discovery

The art of teaching is the art of assisting discovery.

MARK VAN DOREN

The larger the island of knowledge,
the longer the shoreline of wonder.

RALPH W. SOCKMAN

We need to recapture the power of imagination;
we shall find that life can be full of wonder,
mystery, beauty, and joy.

SIR HAROLD SPENCER JONES

The hopes of the godly result in happiness.

PROVERBS 10:28 NLT

To learn is to change.
Education is a process that changes the learner.

GEORGE B. LEONARD

....

....

....

....

....

....

*You cannot teach others anything.
You can only help them to discover
it within themselves.*

GALILEO GALILEI

The Extra Mile

Teaching is an exhausting job.
I did not, however, expect to be emotionally exhausted.
I suppose the easiest way out of this dilemma
would be to make myself emotionally unavailable
to my students.... Not this teacher.
This teacher can't help but share in some
of those emotional moments.
I can't turn off a portion of myself when
I walk into the classroom. It's either all of me or nothing.

ALLISON L. BAER

Going far beyond the call of duty,
doing more than others expect...
is what excellence is all about.
And it comes from striving,
maintaining the highest standards,
looking after the smallest detail,
and going the extra mile.
Excellence means doing your very best.
In everything. In every way.

Whatever you give is acceptable if you give it eagerly. And give according to what you have, not what you don't have.

2 CORINTHIANS 8:12 NLT

A Childlike Attitude

One should take children's philosophy to heart.
They do not despise a bubble because it bursts.
They immediately set to work to blow another one.

Only a child can see any value in rain puddles.

A young child, a fresh,
uncluttered mind, a world before him—
to what treasures will you lead him?

GLADYS M. HUNT

Anyone who welcomes a little child
like this on My behalf welcomes Me,
and anyone who welcomes Me
welcomes...My Father who sent Me.

MARK 9:37 NLT

You know children are growing up when they start asking questions that have answers.

J. J. PLOMP

Helping Hands

Remember, if you ever need a helping hand,
you'll find one at the end of your arm.
As you grow older, you will discover that
you have two hands, one for helping yourself,
the other for helping others.

SAM LEVENSON

Sympathize with each other.
Love each other as brothers and sisters.
Be tenderhearted, and keep a humble attitude.

1 PETER 3:8 NLT

Service is the rent we each pay for living.
It is not something to do in your spare time;
it is the very purpose of life.

MARIAN WRIGHT EDELMAN

A little thing is a little thing, but faithfulness in a little thing is a big thing.

HUDSON TAYLOR

Kindness

The attitudes of teachers and students
have the greatest influence on learning....
Inspiring students with a sense of their own worth
gives them the confidence to express themselves
more freely, to explore and learn through their mistakes,
and to regard learning as an adventure....
The teacher's kind disposition, aside from being
a good educational tool, has an importance beyond
the mere teaching of subject matter. The demonstration
of love, understanding, and forgiveness is a human
lesson profoundly vital to the education of
each pupil in growth toward maturity and humanity.

JAY SOMMER

How precious is Your lovingkindness,
O God! And the children of men take refuge
in the shadow of Your wings.

PSALM 36:7 NASB

We think of the effective teachers we have had over the years with a sense of recognition, but those who have touched our humanity we remember with a deep sense of gratitude.

On Education

Upon the subject of education,
not presuming to dictate any plan or system
respecting it, I can only say that I view it as
the most important subject which
we as a people may be engaged in.
That everyone may receive at least
a moderate education appears to be
an objective of vital importance.

ABRAHAM LINCOLN

Our progress as a nation can be
no swifter than our progress in education.
The human mind is our fundamental resource.

JOHN F. KENNEDY

God has given each of us the ability
to do certain things well. So...if you are a teacher,
do a good job of teaching.

ROMANS 12:6–7 TLB

....

....

....

....

....

....

*The most important educational experience
happening to students is their teacher.*

VIRGIL E. HERRICK

Hard Work

Don't be afraid to give your best
to what seemingly are small jobs.
Every time you conquer one it makes you
that much stronger. If you do the little jobs well,
the big ones will tend to take care of themselves.

DALE CARNEGIE

The price of success is hard work,
dedication to the job at hand,
and the determination that whether
we win or lose, we have applied the best
of ourselves to the task at hand....
The quality of a person's life is in
direct proportion to their commitment to excellence,
regardless of their chosen field of endeavor.

VINCENT T. LOMBARDI

Now he who plants and he who waters are one, and each one will receive his own reward according to his own labor.

What We Reap

Often, when I am reading a good book,
I stop and thank my teacher.
That is, I used to, until she got an unlisted number.

We were doing a science lesson on how plants grow.
The children all got a chance to plant their own seeds.
As the teacher, I planted a few extra seeds
for the children whose plants might not sprout.
After a few weeks of watching them,
I secretly exchanged a few. The next day
one of my students said, "Look, Teacher.
It's a miracle! My plant is growing."
I said, "Yes, seeds sprouting is very exciting."
He said, "No, Teacher, that's not the miracle.
I ate the seed and it's growing anyway!"

DEBBIE CAPUANO

....

....

....

....

....

....

....

....

Let us not lose heart in doing good,
for in due time we will reap
if we do not grow weary.

GALATIANS 6:9 NASB

Love One Another

Let me be a little kinder,
Let me be a little blinder
To the faults of those about me;
Let me praise a little more.
Let me be, when I am weary,
Just a little bit more cheery;
Let me serve a little better
Those that I am striving for.

Let me be a little braver
When temptation bids me waver;
Let me strive a little harder
To be all that I should be.
Let me be a little meeker
With my brother who is weeker;
Let me think more of my neighbor
And a little less of me.

Be kind to one another, tenderhearted,
forgiving one another.

EPHESIANS 4:32 NKJV

The Work God Does

"Of all who live, I am the one by whom
This work can best be done in the right way."
Then shall I see it not too great, nor small,
To suit my spirit; and to prove my power;
Then shall I cheerful greet the laboring hours,
And cheerful turn when the long shadows fall
At eventide, to play and love and rest,
Because I know for me my work is best.

HENRY VAN DYKE

It is not the work we do that is so important.
It's the people we work with.
It's the work God does in our lives
through them. And it's the work
He does in their lives through us.
That is what's sacred.

KEN GIRE

....

....

....

....

....

....

....

*It is good for people to...enjoy their work...
and to accept their lot in life.*

ECCLESIASTES 5:18 NLT

Little by Little

Keep on sowing your seed, for you never know
which will grow—perhaps it all will.

ECCLESIASTES 11:6 TLB

You climb a long ladder until you can see
over the roof, or over the clouds....
You watch your shod feet step on
each round rung, one at a time;
you do not hurry and do not rest....
You climb steadily, doing your job in the dark.
When you reach the end,
there is nothing more to climb.
The sun hits you. The bright wideness
surprises you; you had forgotten
there was an end. You look back at
the ladder's two feet on the distant grass, astonished.

ANNIE DILLARD

Remember that your work comes only moment by moment, and as surely as God calls you to work, He gives the strength to do it.

PRISCILLA MAURICE

Commit to a Dream

Most people think I am a dreamer....
We need visions for larger things,
for the unfolding and reviewing of worthwhile things.

MARY McLEOD BETHUNE

The important thing really is not
the deed well done or the medal that you possess,
but the dedication and dreams out of which they grow.

ROBERT H. BENSON

Commit yourself to a dream....
Nobody who tries to do something great
but fails is a total failure. Why?
Because they can always rest assured
that they succeeded in life's most important battle—
they defeated the fear of trying.

ROBERT SCHULLER

....

....

....

....

....

....

....

*You are God! Your words are trustworthy,
and You have promised these good things.*

2 SAMUEL 7:28 NIV

Learning for a Lifetime

Through my students—over all those years—
I learned what I know about unselfish love,
about laughter, about sharing, about questioning,
about honest, no-nonsense study. I learned
the joy of losing oneself in the magic
of the classroom encounter.... You will have
memories that won't stop. Your mind will
have been challenged; your values will have been
forged into potent tools; you will feel a kind
of satisfaction that you did your bit for your world:
you showed up—in a most meaningful way.

BARBARA GOLEMAN

Truth, righteousness, peace, faith,
and salvation are more than words.
Learn how to apply them.
You'll need them throughout your life.

EPHESIANS 6:14–15 MSG

I appreciate now how life can be a school.
Wherever I go, whatever I do,
I can learn and grow and
contribute. I learned that from you.

Ellie Claire℠ Gift & Paper Corp.
Minneapolis 55438
www.ellieclaire.com

Words to Warm a Teacher's Heart Journal
© 2012 Ellie Claire Gift & Paper Corp
ellieclaire.com

ISBN 978-1-60936-606-3

Compiled by Marilyn Jansen
Cover and Interior Design by Jeff and Lisa Franke

Printed in China.